WYE VALLEY 1

This guide book contains exact but simple directions for ... combine visits to such well known places as Chepstow, Raglan, Monmouth, Symonds Yat, or Ross, with an exploration of the small towns and villages of the Wye Valley and the Forest of Dean, that lie hidden beyond the network of busy main roads.

The 'Main Circle' Route (Map 1–11) shown on the Key Map covers 118 miles, most of which are through quiet unspoilt country. This route can be approached with ease from Birmingham, Worcester, Hereford, Abergavenny, Newport, Bristol and Gloucester. You will find that the strip maps show the 'A' roads approaching from the towns, thus giving you an easy link with 'civilization'.

The 'Main Circle' Route (Map 1–11) is rather too long for a leisurely day's journey, and we have included 'Link Routes' to break this up into smaller circles. The 'North Circle' starts from Ross and uses Maps 4–5–6–7–8–9 to Raglan, from whence a return may be made to Ross on the A40. The 'South Circle' consists of Maps 1–2–3–4–12–13–14–7–8–9–10–11. The 'South-West Circle' consists of Maps 1–15–13–14–7–8–9–10–11.

It should be stressed that each route, being circular, may be started at any point, and that a break can be made anywhere you wish to visit a nearby town for lunch, or to stay in a hotel for the night. You will find directions for doing this clearly marked on the borders of the strip maps, and although mileages are not shown, these can easily be worked out by reference to the Key Map opposite.

HOW TO USE YOUR BOOK ON THE ROUTE

Each double page makes up a complete picture of the country ahead of you. On the left you will find a one inch to the mile strip map, with the route marked by a series of dashes. Direction is always from top to bottom, so that the map may be looked at in conjunction with the 'directions to the driver', with which it is cross referenced by a letter itemising each junction point. This enables the driver to have exact guidance every time an opportunity for changing direction occurs, even if it is only 'Keep straight, not left'!

With mileage intervals shown, the driver should even have warning when to expect these 'moments of decision', and if a sign post exists we have used this to help you, with the 'Follow sign marked...' column. However re-signing is always in progress, and this may lead to slight differences in sign marking in some cases... So beware of freshly erected signs.

We have also included a description of the towns and villages through which you will pass, together with some photographs to illustrate the route.

To gain full enjoyment from these journeys, be prepared to leave your car as often as possible. Walk in forests, and beside rivers, explore old towns, churches and castles. We hope that this guide helps you towards the threshold of discovery... the rest is in your hands.

Compiled by PETER and HELEN TITCHMARSH
Photography by ALAN, PETER and CHRISTOPHER TITCHMARSH

Map 1

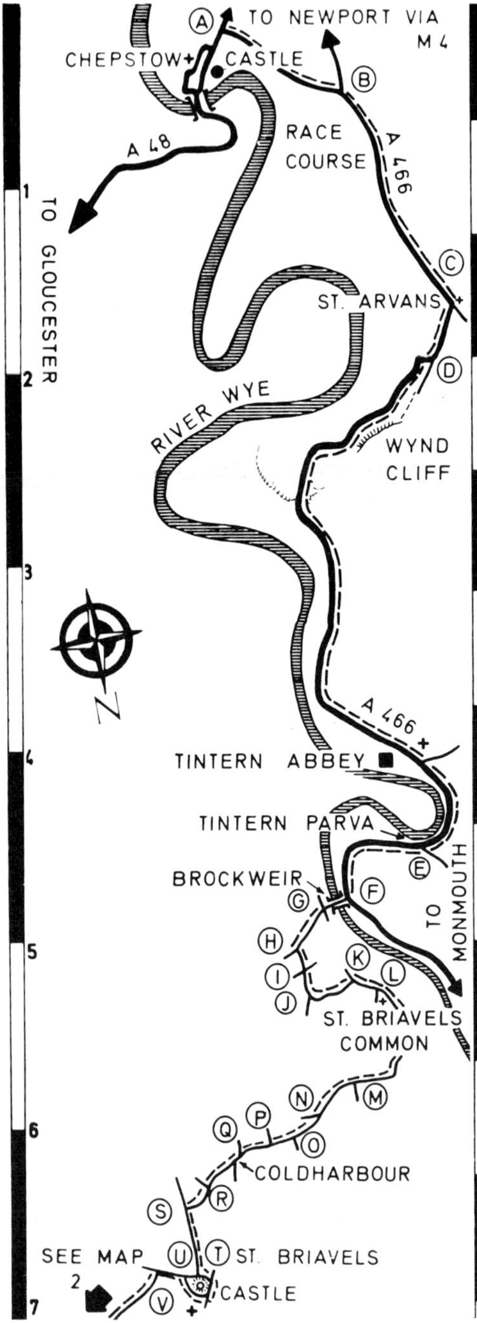

Ref.	kms Miles	Directions	Signposted
A		Start from the Gatehouse, Chepstow, and follow out on A466	'Welsh Street'
B	.8	Turn right at roundabout keeping on A466	Monmouth
C	1.2	Bear right in St. Arvans, keeping on A466	Monmouth
D	.4	Turn right, keeping on A466.	Monmouth
	.5	Car Park for '365 Steps' on left. This is access point for the Wynd Cliff	
	.9	Fine views of Wye through woods on right	
	1.5	Tintern Abbey on right	
		Straight through Tintern on A466	
E	.7	Straight, not left in Tintern Parva. (BUT TURN LEFT AND FOLLOW MAP 15 FOR ROUTE TO MONMOUTH)	No sign
F	.7	Turn right, off A466, and cross Wye	Brockweir
G	.1	Over small X rds., and leave Brockweir	No sign
H	.3	Turn left at T junction	Cold Harbour
I	.3	Over small X rds.	No sign
J	.2	Fork left	St. Briavels Common
K	.2	Turn right at T junction	No sign
L	.1	Straight, not right	No sign
M	1.4	Straight, not left	St. Briavels
N	.1	Fork left	No sign
O	.1	Straight, not left	St. Briavels
P	.2	Straight, not right	No sign
Q	.1	Over off-set X rds. at Coldharbour	No sign
R	.2	Straight, not right	No sign
S	.1	Turn left at T junction on to B4228	St. Briavels
	.2	Enter St. Briavels	
T	.2	Turn left at T junction, and circle ¾ round the Castle, keeping it on your right, with the church on left. Fine views on left	Bigsweir
U	.2	Turn left at T junction beyond Post Office	No sign
V	.2	Turn left at T junction, rejoining on B4228	Coleford
		Total mileage on this map: 10.9	

CROWN COPYRIGHT RESERVED

On Route

Chepstow
This busy market town marks the end of the Wye's 130 mile passage to the sea. It is crossed here by a graceful iron bridge, built in 1816, which is overlooked by the magnificently sited castle.
The massive fifty foot high Norman Keep is itself perched upon the very edge of a sheer cliff rising 90 feet above the muddy banks of the river. Look round this dramatic castle, and marvel at the views it affords of the Wye and the wooded hills that rise beyond.
See also the interesting Museum, opposite the castle car park, the Town Gate, the walls, and the Parish Church with its fine Norman nave and splendid tomb of the 2nd Earl of Worcester.

1. Chepstow Castle

The Wynd Cliff
Massive limestone cliffs towering eight hundred feet above the Wye. There is a path of '365 Steps' from our road (See Route Directions, beyond Point D) climbing steeply through the trees to the highest point. From here there are splendid views out over the Wye, curving round the Lancaut peninsula towards the broad Severn estuary, and the Cotswolds on the distant skyline. Chepstow Castle and the Severn Bridge are easily visible, and on the clearest of days, the tower of Gloucester Cathedral may also be spotted.
Coming here in 1833, the architect Augustus Pugin, never one for under-statement, claimed that he saw four cathedrals and fourteen counties. County boundaries and county names have changed since Pugin's day... Hereford and Worcester are now one, and Avon has sprung up between Gloucestershire and Somerset... but you should still consider yourself fortunate if you can notch up more than six counties, and perhaps two cathedrals. We should be pleased to hear from any readers who feel that they have done better than this.

2. Tintern Abbey

Tintern Abbey
This magnificent Cistercian abbey once covered no less than 27 acres. It was founded in 1131, and though inevitably dissolved in 1535, it became one of England's early tourist attractions, following preservation work started by the Beaufort family in 1756. Gain a fascinating insight into monastic life by visiting these sympathetically preserved buildings, and if possible, climb the hill to the little Parish Church, to appreciate the genius of the Cistercians in their choice of the Abbey's site, and in its final design.

3. The Wye at Brockweir

Brockweir
Attractive hamlet approached by an unusually ugly bridge. The Wye ceases to be tidal here.

St. Briavels
Small town perched 700 feet above the Wye, with the remains of a 13th century castle. This was once the administrative centre of the Forest of Dean, and is now a Youth Hostel. See the castle gateway, the interesting Norman church, and the lovely sylvan views westward over the Wye.

4. St. Briavels Castle and Church

Map 2

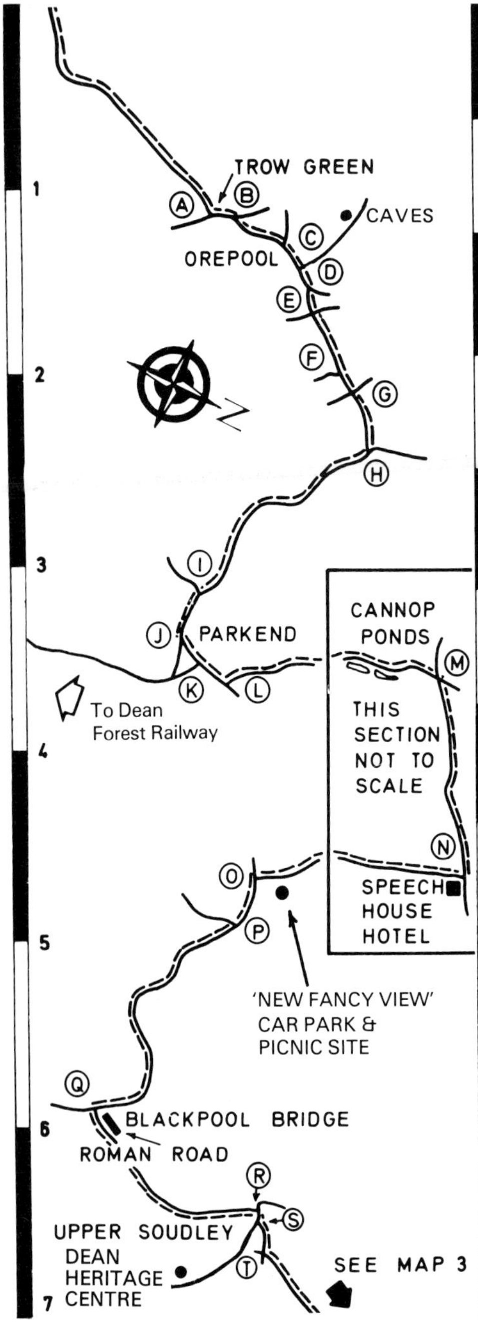

Miles	kms Ref. Miles	Directions	Sign-posted
	.9	Enter National Forest Park area, but not apparent yet	
A	1.1	Straight, not right at Trow Green	Coleford
B	.1	Straight, not left at Trow Green	Coleford
C	.3	Straight, not left at Orepool	Coleford
D	.3	Turn right at T junction	Parkend
E	.1	Over X rds.	Parkend
F	.4	Straight, not right	No sign
G	.1	Over small X rds.	Parkend
H	.4	Turn right on to B4431	Parkend
I	1.4	Straight, not right	Parkend
J	.2	Fork left	Blakeney
K	.1	Straight, not right (But turn right on to B4234 for the Dean Forest Railway, Steam Centre... on right after 3 miles)	Blakeney
L	.2	Turn left at T junction, on to B4234	Lydbrook
	1.3	1st of the Cannop Ponds on right (Waymarked Nature Trail on right)	
	.6	2nd of Cannop Ponds on right	
M	.4	Turn right on to B4226, by Wood Distillery	Cinderford
	.5	Up steep hill	
N	.3	Turn right by the Speech House Hotel	Parkend
	.2	Speech House Arboretum and car park down to left... incorporates the Spruce Ride... a fine avenue just visible from road	
	1.6	'New Fancy View' car park and picnic site on left	
O	.3	Turn left at T junction on to B4431	Yorkley
P	.3	Straight, not right	Blakeney
	.7	Pleasant forest country here... Oak, Beech, Silver Birches, and a stream on right	
Q	.9	Turn left at T junction, at Blackpool Bridge	Soudley
	.1	Exposed stretch of Roman Road on left	
	.8	Forest path to Stapledge on left	
R	.4	Turn right, and almost immediately...	Blakeney
S	.1	Straight, not right (But keep right, on B4227 for half a mile, following signs to the Dean Heritage Centre, if you wish to visit this worthwhile place [See page 7])	No sign
T	.2	Turn left at small X rds.	Little Dean
		Total mileage on this map: 14.3	

CROWN COPYRIGHT RESERVED

On Route

Forest of Dean
The Forest has a long and complex connection with the Crown, but in 1924 it was transferred to the Forestry Commission, who now have over 20,000 acres carrying trees. In 1931 it became England's first National Forest Park, and the interests of visitors allow the economic requirements of the Commission very closely indeed.

The Forest occupies a plateau (about 500 feet high) in a triangle between Gloucester, Ross and Chepstow. Its great tracts of woodland are punctuated by small coal mines, and the remains of many iron workings (scowles), but only in a few places do they spoil the visitors enjoyment. The towns and villages that border the forest are, with a few exceptions, not specially beautiful. If our route takes you past bare ugliness from time to time, bear with us, and save your eyes for the trees and the splendid views of blue green hills and mountain silhouettes beyond.

Roads through the Forest are good, but do not let this tempt you to pass through too quickly. Leave your car and walk into the trees as far, and as often as possible. If you require more detailed information on every aspect of Dean Forest, see note on Forest Trails, etc. on Page 7.

1. At Cannop Ponds

Clearwell Caves Iron Mines
An interesting old iron mine with local mining and geological exhibits and several vintage stationary engines. Turn left in Orepool, beyond Point C.

Parkend
This is definitely not our favourite forest village, and is a scrappy, rather indeterminate place. The northern terminus of the Dean Forest Railway is here, but turn right at Point K, and drive three miles southwards on B4234 for the Forest Railway's 'Steam Centre' at New Mills, Lydney. This is a working railway museum, with full sized locomotives and rolling stock, and steam train rides north to Parkend on certain days.

2. The Road to Speech House

Cannop Ponds
A pleasant area to stop awhile, if not too crowded. The Nature Trail is well worth following, especially if you have children with you.

Speech House
Built between 1668 and 1680, Speech House became the centre of the Forest administration in succession to St. Briavels Castle (See Page 3). It is now a hotel, but the Verderer's Court still meets here each spring, a survival of the appointment of Verderers made by Canute in 1016. There is a 2½ mile Forest Trail starting and finishing here, and a descriptive booklet is available from the hotel.

New Fancy View
This is a pleasant car park and picnic area, with a well sited view-point... all within an imaginatively landscaped area created from old coal-mine waste tips. There is a 3½ mile Forest Trail starting and finishing here.

3. Speech House

Roman Road, Blackpool Bridge (See Page 7)

4. Roman Road at Blackpool Bridge

Map 3

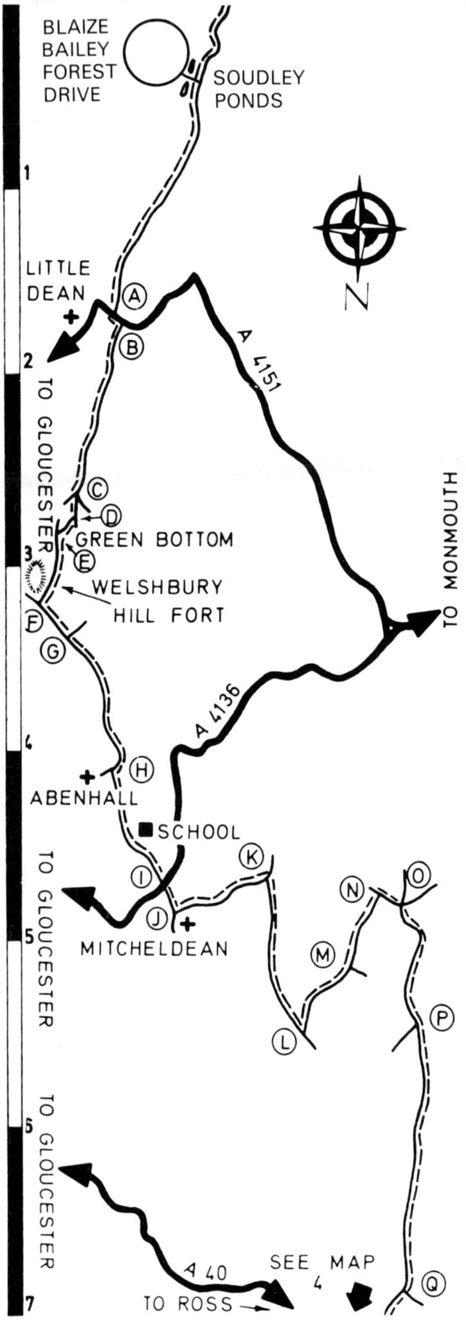

	kms Ref. Miles	Directions	Sign-posted
	.5	Groups of trees on left, named on sign boards by Forestry Commission, including many tall Douglas Firs.	
	.2	Blaize Bailey viewpoint, car park, picnic place and forest drive on right. Do not miss this	
		Leave the Forest	
	1.4	Enter Little Dean	
A	.1	Turn left on to A4151	Cinderford
B	.1	Turn right by the George Hotel	Flaxley
	.7	Re-enter the Forest	
C	.3	Take centre of three fork roads	Green Bottom
D	.1	Fork right	No sign
	.1	Through Green Bottom hamlet	
E	.1	Turn left	No sign
	.3	Welshbury Hill Fort above on right	
F	.1	Turn left at T junction	Micheldean
G	.4	Straight, not left	No sign
H	.7	Turn left, (but go straight to visit Abenhall church)	No sign
	.4	Abenhall School on left	
	.3	Enter Mitcheldean	
I		Over X rds. crossing A4136	Ross
J	.2	Turn left just before church	Drybrook
	.2	Up steep hill out of Mitcheldean	
K	.4	Turn right	Wigpool
L	1.0	Turn sharp left at T junction	No sign
M	.4	Straight, not right, by phone box	No sign
N	.5	Turn right at T junction	No sign
O	.1	Turn right at X rds onto busier road	No sign
	.3	Descend hill. Fine views over to left	
P	.4	Straight, not right	Ross
	.1	Leaving Forest Park	
	.4	Malvern Hills visible on skyline	
Q	1.0	Straight, not left	Ross
		Total mileage on this map: 10.8	

CROWN COPYRIGHT RESERVED

On Route

Roman Road, Blackpool Bridge (See Page 4)
Here is an exposed and carefully restored stretch of Roman road. Constructed in the first or second century A.D., it ran from Lydney to Mitcheldean. The marks of wheeled traffic are clearly visible on the roughly paved surface.

Dean Heritage Centre (See page 4)
Just off our route, and set around a tranquil mill pond, the heritage of the Forest of Dean is portrayed here through museum displays and an audio-visual presentation. There is a cafe, craft shop and adventure playground.

1. At Soudley Ponds

Upper Soudley
Our road beyond Map 2, Point T, passes through some very attractive forest country, with many of the wide variety of trees named on signboards. See Route Directions for access to the Blaize Bailey View-Point, which is reached by way of a circular Forest Drive, complete with car park and picnic area. The nearby Abbots Wood Forest Trail (3 miles) passes the attractive Soudley Ponds, which are themselves visible from our road.

Forest Trails
There are about a dozen Forest Trails in Dean Forest, to many of which we refer in our text and route directions. These trails are all waymarked with red arrows and particular spots are marked with numbers which refer to details in the relevant Forestry Commission booklets, and it is essential to have these to understand the trails. Some booklets are obtainable at the start of the trails (e.g. at Speech House Hotel, Christchurch Camp Site), but to obtain individual booklets or a complete set, write enclosing a stamped and addressed envelope, to *The Forestry Commission, Forest Trails, Crown Office, Coleford, Glos. GL16 8BA*, who will send you a list of these very modestly priced booklets.

2. Little Dean Church

Little Dean
A large village at the foot of the Dean Forest plateau, with few features of interest. The church has a pleasant enough Perpendicular tower. Its interior is rather bare, being relieved only by the ornamental bosses of the oak roof and some pleasing 18th century wall tablets.

3. The Road to Green Bottom

Abenhall
A few houses and a church, all lying well back from our road. Although over restored in the 19th century, Abenhall church retains an interesting flavour, with a 15th century octagonal font, two sides of which depict the arms of the Free Miners, and the Free Smiths, alongside the arms of the local gentry in the other six panels.

Mitcheldean
This town has, in the past, rather let itself go, but it appears to be recovering considerably, and judging from the piano music echoing across the square from the George, when we once called here, there's life in Mitcheldean yet! *Continued on Page 9*

4. In Abenhall Churchyard

Map 4

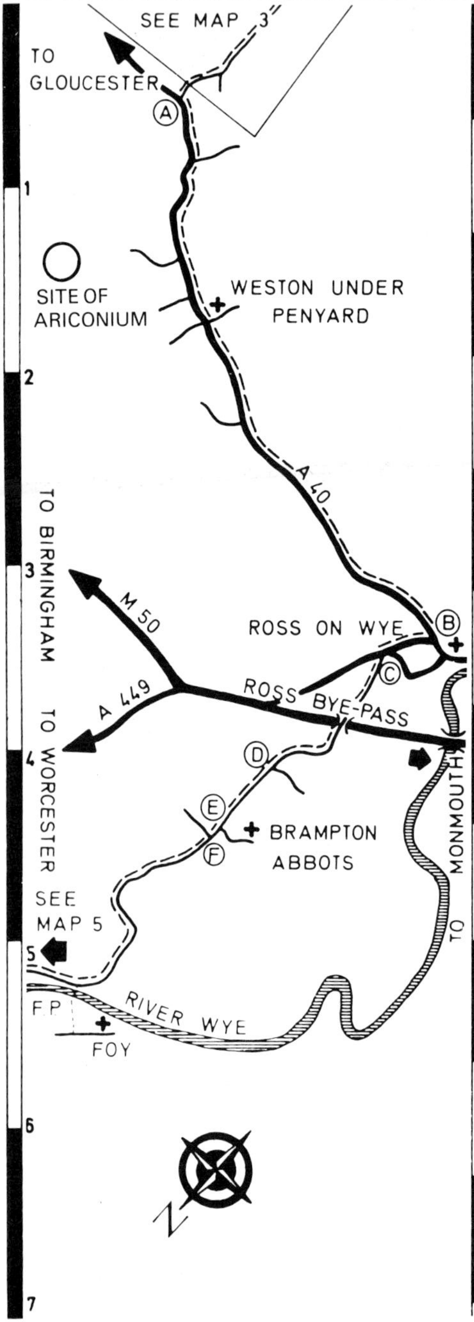

Ref	kms/Miles	Directions	Sign-posted
A	.3	Bear left on to A40 (Keep on A40 for 2½ miles until reaching Ross)	Ross
	.5	Baptist Chapel on right	
	.4	Weston-under-Penyard entry signed	
	.3	Weston Cross Inn on right	
	1.0	Ross church spire visible ahead	
	.5	Enter Ross on Wye (Keep on A40 into centre)	
B*	.8	Turn right by Market Hall on to A449 (Unless you wish to visit church. In which case, go straight and turn left by Lloyds Bank)	Ledbury
		*For alternative route from this point, turn to Map 12, Point A	
C	.2	Fork left by the Transport Hotel	Brampton Abbotts
		Follow out of town on this road	
	.4	Cross bridge over By-pass	
D	.5	Straight, not left	No sign
E	.5	Straight, not left	Ledbury
		But turn left to visit Brampton Abbotts church	
F	.1	Straight, not right	Foy
	1.1	Down steep hill. River Wye visible ahead	
	.2	Miniature suspension bridge on left. Walk across here and over the fields to Foy	
		Total mileage on this map: 6.8	

CROWN COPYRIGHT RESERVED

On Route

Mitcheldean *Continued from Page 7*

The church has a most graceful 15th century spire, and an unusually wide nave. The Norman font has the twelve apostles ranged round its surface and the rugged simplicity of its carving makes a startling contrast with the elaborate 19th century reredos in grey marble. The latter may not have much warmth, but one must admire the sheer quality and quantity of technical skill devoted to it.

Weston-under-Penyard

A small tidy village lying beneath the wooded slopes of Penyard Hill, with a pleasant inn, the 'Weston Cross'. The church looks out over the village and has a sensible, well proportioned 14th century tower and a wooden north porch of about the same age. The Norman arcading is very pleasing, being both stout and well ornamented. The wall tablets bring a touch of 18th century elegance to the otherwise simple interior.

Weston Hall, a fine 17th century house in red sandstone, has an attractively gabled porch and splendid early 18th century gates on to our road. To the north east of the village, is the site of the Roman settlement of ARICONIUM, which lay on the Roman road running from Lydney to Ashton near Leominster, the remains of which we have already seen at Blackpool Bridge (See Page 7). Although it has been twice excavated, there is now nothing to be seen of the ARICONIUM site.

Ross-on-Wye

Busy market town and chief tourist centre of the Wye Valley, Ross should be visited out of high season to be truly appreciated. Its streets and shops are full of character, and activity centres on the 17th century Market Hall of red sandstone. This pleasant building escaped the 19th century improvers who filled in so many ground-level arcades in various parts of the country, and lively market stalls are still set up here each week.

Climbing up from the Market Hall, one reaches the Churchyard, bordered on the north side by delightful 17th century houses, and on the west by 'The Prospect', a pleasant garden leased to the town for 500 years by John Kyrle, the 'Man of Ross'. Here one can sit in the sun and look down on the Wye curving beneath the town, and on towards Wilton Bridge (1599), and the ruins of Wilton Castle.

The splendid church spire is best seen from Wilton Bridge, or from the meadows between M50 and the town. The 19th century restorers have left their mark on the interior, but the elaborate Rudhall tombs are well worth inspecting.

Brampton Abbotts

Rudhall House dates from the early 14th century, but it is more notable for its fine 16th century timberwork. This was the home of the Rudhall family (See Ross-on-Wye above) and there is an attractive little

Continued on Page 11

Foy (See Page 11)

1. Houses by the Churchyard, Ross

2. Wilton Bridge, near Ross

3. Brampton Abbotts Church

4. Footbridge to Foy

Map 5

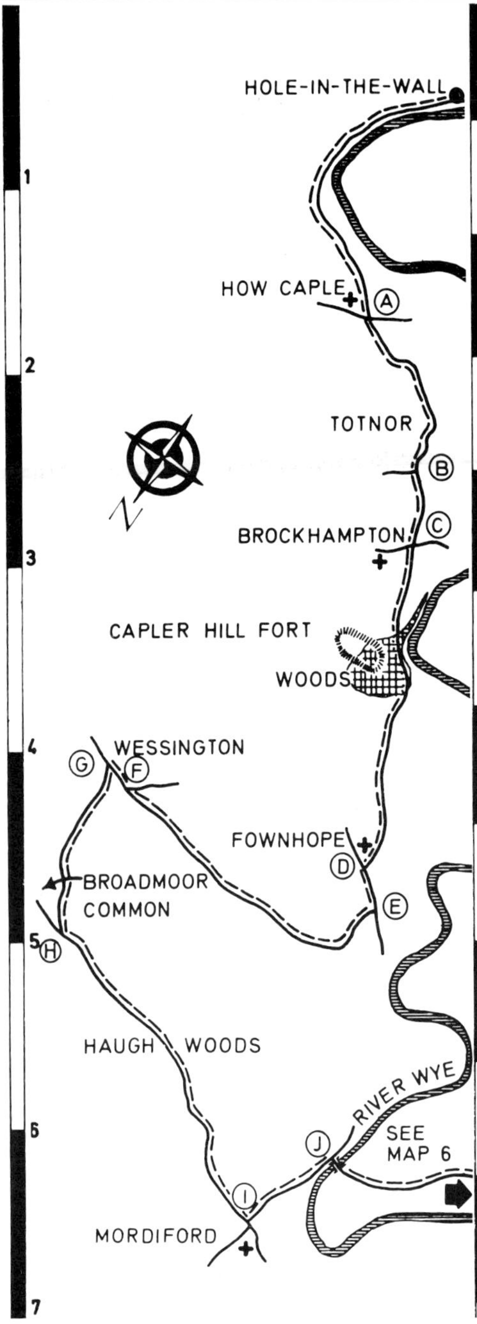

	kms Ref. Miles	Directions	Sign-posted
	.4	Through hamlet of 'Hole in the Wall'	
	.3	Through open meadowland, which slopes down to the Wye, with woods on left	
	1.3	How Caple House visible through trees on right	
A	.3	Over X rds. (But turn right, and right again to visit How Caple church)	Fownhope
	.8	Through hamlet of Totnor	
B	.2	Straight, not right	No sign
C	.4	Over X rds. (But turn right to visit Brockhampton church)	Fownhope
	.4	Enter Capler Woods. Wonderful views down towards the Wye on left. Earthworks of Capler Camp not visible, but lie above, right	
	1.3	Enter Fownhope	
D	.1	Turn left at T junction by the church, on to the B4224	Hereford
		Note: Old milestone on corner of churchyard wall	
E	.3	Turn right at offset at X rds	Woolhope
F	1.7	Straight, not right	No sign
G	.2	Turn left at T junction by half timbered farm, at Wessington hamlet	No sign
	.8	Broadmoor Common on right	
H	.1	Bear left at T junction	Hereford
	.2	Enter Haugh Wood	
	1.5	Enter Mordiford	
I	.3	Turn left at T junction by the Moon Inn, on to B4224. (But turn right to visit church and to look at bridge over the Lugg)	Fownhope
J	.6	Turn right and cross over River Wye. Bridge not very attractive, but the river here with its sandy shallows and grassy banks is the Wye at its very best	Holme Lacy
		Total mileage on this map: 11.2	

On Route

Brampton Abbotts *Continued from Page 9*
...ass to 'Joan Rudhale' in the church. This building has a 14th century timbered porch which has been rebuilt, a timbered bell turret, and Norman features including nave, chancel and south doorway.

Foy (See Page 8)
For walkers only, but well worthwhile. Foy church and vicarage look out over the Wye, the former containing a fine roof and chancel screen.

1. The Wye near 'Hole-in-the-Wall'

Low Caple
The church stands below the court, on the edge of wooded parkland sloping down towards the Wye, a good mile from the rest of this minute village. It has a fine tower, but its plain exterior gives no clue to its contents, which include a splendid chancel screen and pulpits, put there by Sir William Gregory, Speaker of the House, in the late 17th century. Over the screen is a handsome carving of the arms of William III. Modern woodwork and glass complete a most satisfactory interior.

Brockhampton
The church was built in 1902 by W. R. Lethaby, an early 'functionalist', who seldom put his ideas to work. The thatched roof and creeper-covered stone tower are moderately pleasing, but the dramatic pointed arches and clean design of the interior are quite exceptional. Such details as the tapestry panels on either side of the altar, and the carvings on the pulpit and stalls, bring warmth of feeling to the 'functional' stonework. Do not miss this unique church.

2. Brockhampton Church

Fownhope
Pleasant village lying between the Wye and wooded hillsides, with a mixture of half-timbered and stone cottages, and a well known inn, 'The Green Man'. The interior of the church suffered considerably in the 19th century, and has scraped walls and highly coloured tiles. However we suggest that you walk up the pleasant flower bordered pathway to the north door, to look at Fownhope's splendid Norman tympanum. This is set in the west wall and depicts the Madonna and Child, with a winged lion on one side and an eagle on the other.

3. View from Capler Woods

Mordiford
A six hundred year old, nine arched bridge here spans the Lugg, a few hundred yards above its confluence with the Wye. If traffic is not too heavy it is pleasant to look upstream, past the rectory garden and the willows, to the lush water meadows beyond. Mordiford church has a Norman south doorway and a much restored Victorian interior. However do not miss the attractive little wall monument to a lady who *died at her prayers in the form as you see her portrature* in the year 1635.
The lordship of the manor here is held on condition that the king is presented with a pair of gilt spurs whenever he crosses Mordiford Bridge. However we have not been able to ascertain if any king has ever come this way to claim his due.

4. The Lugg above Mordiford Bridge

Map 6

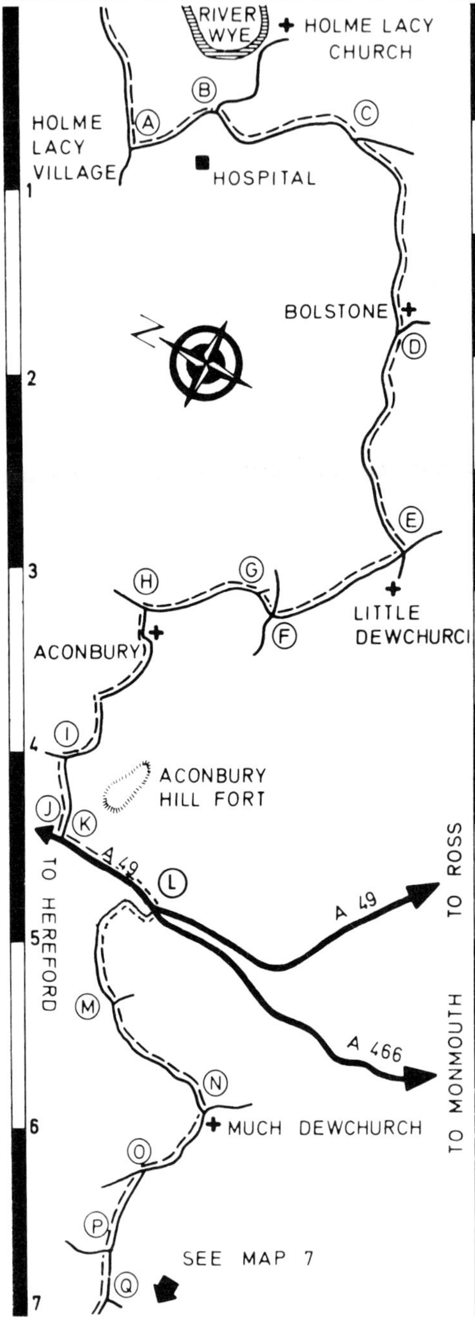

Ref.	kms	Miles	Directions	Sign-posted
		.9	Enter Holme Lacy	
A		.4	Turn left at T junction	Bolstone
		.3	Entrance to Holme Lacy Hospital on right	
B		.2	Straight, not left at T junction (But turn left to visit Holme Lacy church)	Bolstone
C	1.0		Straight, not left at T junction	Bolstone
	1.1		Bolstone hamlet on left, with small church behind farm buildings… easily missed from the road	
D		.1	Turn right at T junction by pond	No sign
		.4	Woods on right	
		.8	Enter Little Dewchurch	
E		.1	Turn right at X rds. (But go straight over to visit church)	Aconbury
F		.9	Over X rds.	Hereford
G		.1	Straight, not right	No sign
H		.7	Turn left at T junction, by bus stop	No sign
		.2	Through Aconbury hamlet. Church on left	
		.7	Aconbury Woods on left. Hill fort hidden by trees	
I		.4	Bear left at T junction by farm	No sign
J		.3	Turn left with great care on to A49	Ross
K		.2	Straight, not left	No sign
L		.5	Fork right, on to A466, and immediately…	Wormelow
			Turn right on to smaller road running back parallel with A49 for a short distance	No sign
M		.8	Fork right	No sign
		.4	Lowe Farm on right	
		.4	Enter Much Dewchurch	
N		.1	Turn right at T junction by church	No sign
			Black Swan Inn on right	
O		.5	Fork left	Kilpeck
P		.4	Straight, not right	No sign
Q		.3	Straight, not left	No sign
			Total mileage on this map: 12.2	

CROWN COPYRIGHT RESERVED

On Route

Holme Lacy

The village is undistinguished, and magnificent Holme Lacy House is now a mental hospital, but the little church in the Wye meadows provides compensation in plenty. Undisturbed by the Victorians, it has carved medieval stalls and a magnificent series of Scudamore tombs; notably those of Sir John Scudamore and his wife (1570) and James Scudamore (1668). Do not miss the modern bronze memorial outside the east end of the church, and the lovely wrought iron gates beyond.

1. Holme Lacy Church

Bolstone

Minute hamlet with a re-built Norman church situated in its well used farmyard.

Little Dewchurch

Rather dull village, relieved by its setting amongst perfect, pastoral countryside, with views southwards towards the Forest of Dean. In the churchyard there is a medieval cross, believed to be contemporary with the 14th century tower; all that remains of the original church.

2. The Road from Bolstone

Aconbury

The church was built between 1230 and 1240 by Austin nuns, who had a priory here, although no trace of the monastic building remains. The beautiful 15th century timber porch has open traceried sides, with angels holding shields... all in wood. This porch was badly in need of repair when we called.
The hamlet is delightfully situated beneath Aconbury Hill (topped by a large Iron Age hill fort), but it is sad to see its half-timbered buildings standing so neglected by the road side.

3. Near Aconbury

Much Dewchurch

The 14th century tower of the church is capped with a high saddleback roof, giving it the flavour of a French chateau. The Norman interior is over-restored, but do not miss the exceedingly handsome wall monument to Walter Pye, Attorney General in James I's reign, which overlooks the altar tomb of his ancestors, John and Walter Pye.
We loved the unspoiled atmosphere of the timbered 'Black Swan', where we were made welcome with steak pie, bread and cheese, and some excellent bitter.

4. Much Dewchurch

Map 7

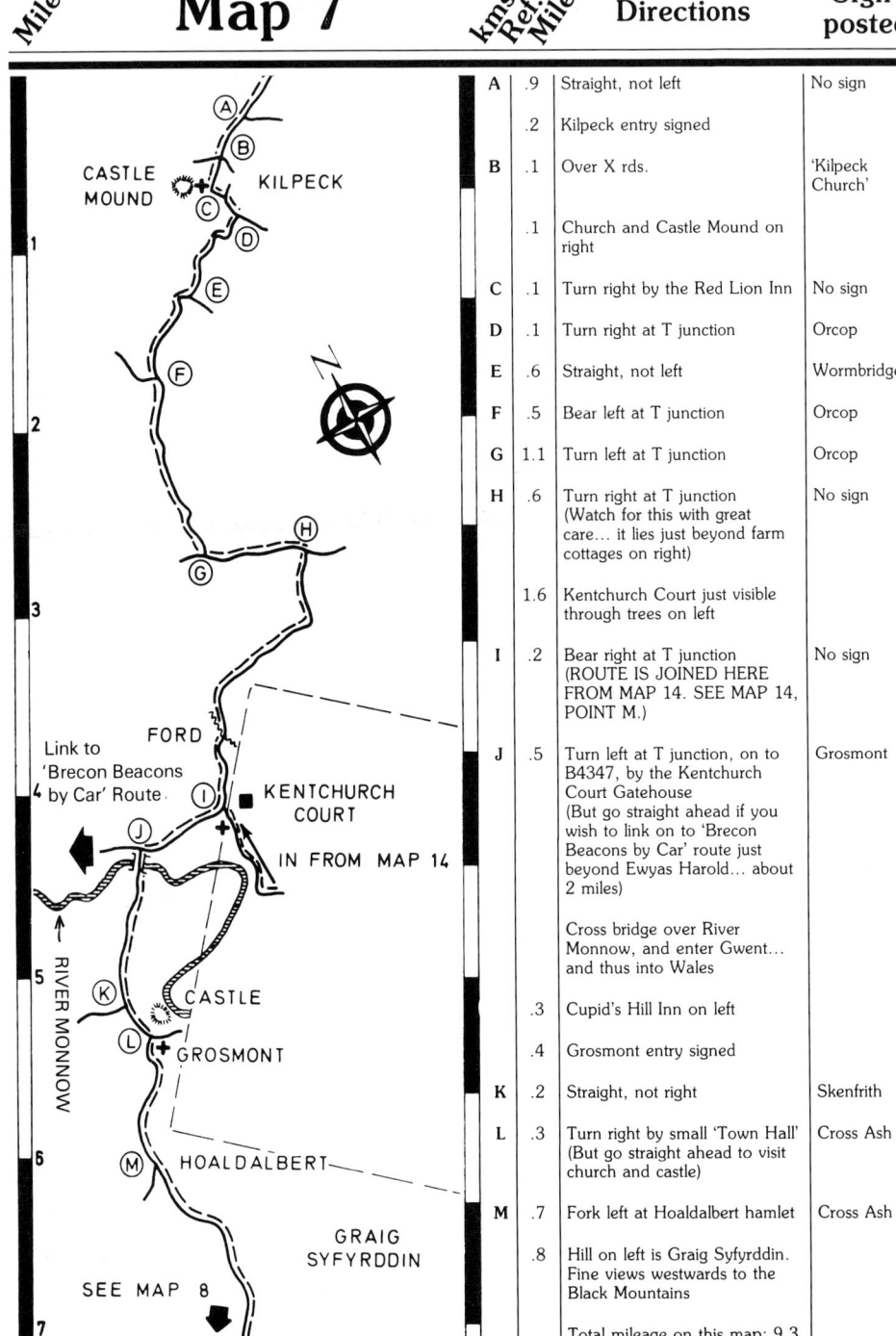

Ref.	kms/Miles	Directions	Sign-posted
A	.9	Straight, not left	No sign
	.2	Kilpeck entry signed	
B	.1	Over X rds.	'Kilpeck Church'
	.1	Church and Castle Mound on right	
C	.1	Turn right by the Red Lion Inn	No sign
D	.1	Turn right at T junction	Orcop
E	.6	Straight, not left	Wormbridge
F	.5	Bear left at T junction	Orcop
G	1.1	Turn left at T junction	Orcop
H	.6	Turn right at T junction (Watch for this with great care... it lies just beyond farm cottages on right)	No sign
	1.6	Kentchurch Court just visible through trees on left	
I	.2	Bear right at T junction (ROUTE IS JOINED HERE FROM MAP 14. SEE MAP 14, POINT M.)	No sign
J	.5	Turn left at T junction, on to B4347, by the Kentchurch Court Gatehouse (But go straight ahead if you wish to link on to 'Brecon Beacons by Car' route just beyond Ewyas Harold... about 2 miles)	Grosmont
		Cross bridge over River Monnow, and enter Gwent... and thus into Wales	
	.3	Cupid's Hill Inn on left	
	.4	Grosmont entry signed	
K	.2	Straight, not right	Skenfrith
L	.3	Turn right by small 'Town Hall' (But go straight ahead to visit church and castle)	Cross Ash
M	.7	Fork left at Hoaldalbert hamlet	Cross Ash
	.8	Hill on left is Graig Syfyrddin. Fine views westwards to the Black Mountains	
		Total mileage on this map: 9.3	

CROWN COPYRIGHT RESERVED

On Route

Kilpeck

Kilpeck church is one of the finest specimens of Romanesque craftmanship in Britain. Its fascinating style clearly reveals the influence of Scandinavian and Mediterranean culture upon native craftsmen. Kilpeck is a very small church, but everything about it is a pleasure to the eye; from the extraordinary intricacies of the south doorway, to the stark simplicity of the apostles upon the chancel arch, and the great Norman font at the west end.

To the west of the church stand the briar covered earthworks of a small castle, topped by the remains of its keep walls.

1. South Door, Kilpeck   2. Carved Figure, Kilpeck

Kentchurch

Set in a magnificent deer park, Kentchurch Court was largely re-built in 1824 by John Nash, the architect of Buckingham Palace. Earlier remains include a 14th century tower which is said to have provided a hiding place for the Welsh prince, Owen Glendower, whose daughter Alice had married the owner of Kentchurch, Sir John Scudamore.

The church was completely re-built in the 19th century, but it contains the interesting tomb of a later Sir John Scudamore, who died in 1616, aged only 47. He is in full armour, lying on a ledge, with his wife and children below, and the tomb is touchingly inscribed:

> His mournful widow to his worth still debtor
> Built him this tomb, but in her heart a better.

3. The Road to Kentchurch

Grosmont

A borough until 1860, and once Monmouthshire's third largest town, Grosmont never fully recovered from its plunder and firing in 1405 by the charmingly titled squire of Owen Glendower, Rhys the Terrible. Today Grosmont is pleasantly grouped about its ambitious little Market Hall, with the attractive 'Angel Inn' nearby. The church has a spire-capped octagonal tower, and an impressively bare nave with fine arcading. The churchyard was being neatly cropped by sheep when we called last, and the gate secured by binder-twine!

4. Grosmont Castle

Grosmont Castle and 'The Trilateral'

The ruins of Grosmont Castle are mainly 13th and 14th century in origin, and are pleasantly sited on a bluff overlooking the winding Monnow. Grosmont, White Castle (Page 17), and Skenfrith (Page 29) formed a defensive network against incursions from the Welsh on this part of the Border, and were known collectively as 'The Trilateral'. With the establishment of more settled conditions, they lost most of their strategic significance, and by the 16th century all three appear to have fallen into decay.

5. The Sugar Loaf, from our road beyond Grosmont

Map 8

Ref	kms/Miles	Directions	Signposted
A	1.0	Bear left at T junction	Cross Ash
B	.3	Turn right at T junction before school	No sign
C	.9	Over X rds. crossing B4521	Brynderi
D	.5	Over X rds. WITH GREAT CARE	No sign
E	.9	Straight, not left at T junction	Llantillio Crosenny
		The Skirrid Mountain visible ahead	
F	.2	Straight not right, and immediately...	
		Turn right at 2nd T junction	Brynderi School
	.3	Brynderi School on right	
		Keep left	No sign
	.3	White Castle now visible ahead	
G	.2	Fork left	White Castle
	.3	Entrance to White Castle on right	
H	.1	Fork left	No sign
I	1.4	Turn right on to B4233 (Site of moated manor on left here)	No sign
J		Almost immediately, turn left off B4233, and enter Llantillio Crosenny	'The Hostry Inn'
K	.2	Turn right. (But go left for church)	No sign
L	.2	Turn left at X rds. by the Hostry Inn	Raglan
	.1	Cross the River Trothy	
M	.9	Fork left beyond farmhouse	Penrhos
		Earthworks of a castle visible on hill ahead	
N	.4	Turn left at T junction	Penrhos
O	.1	Almost immediately turn right	Penrhos
P	.2	Fork right	No sign
Q	.5	Straight, not left, at Pentwyn	No sign
	.2	Enter small village of Penrhos	
R	.4	Turn left at T junction	No sign
S	.6	Straight, not left	No sign
T	.3	Turn right at T junction (But go left 100 yards to visit Tregare church)	Bryngwyn
	.1	Sugar Loaf Mountain visible ahead	
U	.4	Turn left at X rds.	Raglan
		Total mileage on this map: 11.0	

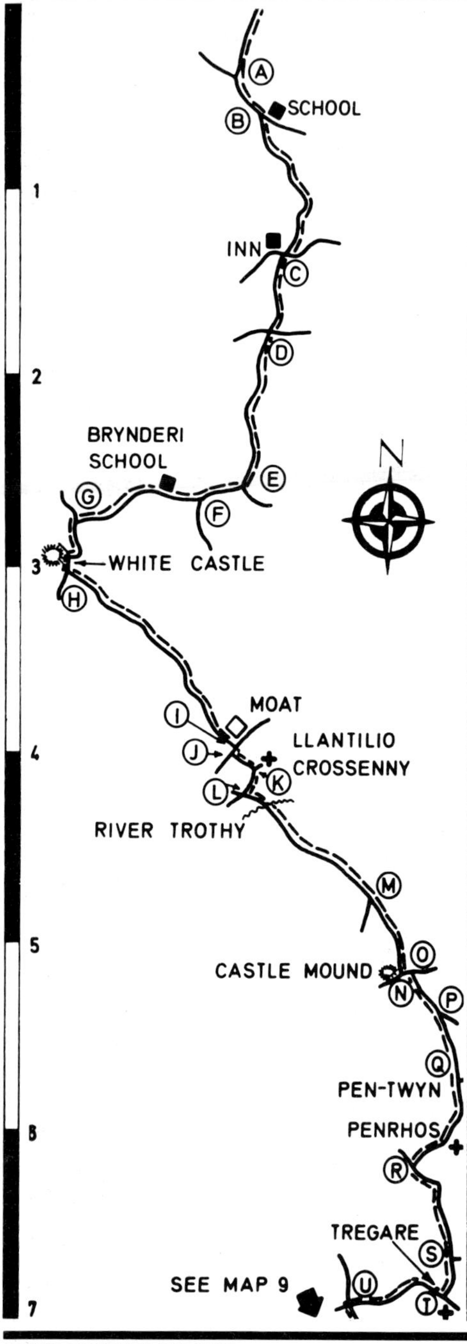

CROWN COPYRIGHT RESERVED

On Route

White Castle

Without doubt the finest of the 'Trilateral' (See page 15), White Castle dominated the roads leading eastwards from the gap in the Welsh hills at Abergavenny. From its high battlements there are wonderful views, north to Graig Syffryddin, west to the Black Mountains, the Skirrid, and the Brecon Beacons and south to Wentwood and Dean Forest.

Saved from stone plunderers by its distance from surrounding villages, White Castle is far more complete than its neighbours. It is most sympathetically preserved and maintained, with well mown lawns and reed bordered moats. Come in early spring, when the air is clear and the grass bordering the moats is enriched with violets and wild daffodils.

Hen Gwrt

The site of a fortified 13th century manor house, surrounded by an attractive reedy moat. Admission free 'at any reasonable time'.

Llantilio Crossenny

Do not miss this most interesting church, with its high nave divided from the chancel by unusually low lower arches. There are three fascinating 17th century floor monuments, and a fine marble relief by Flaxman, depicting in a typically poignant manner, Mrs. Mary Bosanquet on her death-bed surrounded by the grieving members of her family. It is easy to feel that Flaxman often over-stepped the mark in his sentimental approach to these commissions, but his work still tugs at the heart of all but the most cynical of us.

The Hostry Inn (*Sign dated 1459 with great self confidence*) serves good bar-snacks and is a very welcome stopping place, both for motorists on our route, and for walkers traversing the Offa's Dyke Long Distance Footpath. This passes White Castle and Llantilio Crossenny, and follows our road towards Penrhos for about a mile and a half.... just a small part of its long route from the North Wales coast at Prestatyn, to the Severn estuary beyond Chepstow, a distance of over 170 miles.

Penrhos

Small village with simple church, in a pretty churchyard with pollarded limes lining the path to the south door. A particularly rugged row of council houses does not enhance the already limited charms of Penrhos.

Tregare

Has an attractive church on a small ridge, from whence there are fine views westwards to the Sugar Loaf. The little tower is considerably broader at its base that at its top, and the slightly pyramoid effect is most pleasing. Where else can one see such a fine, at, gilded weather-cock on so small a church?

1. White Castle

2. The Moat, Hen Gwrt

3. Tregare Church

Map 9

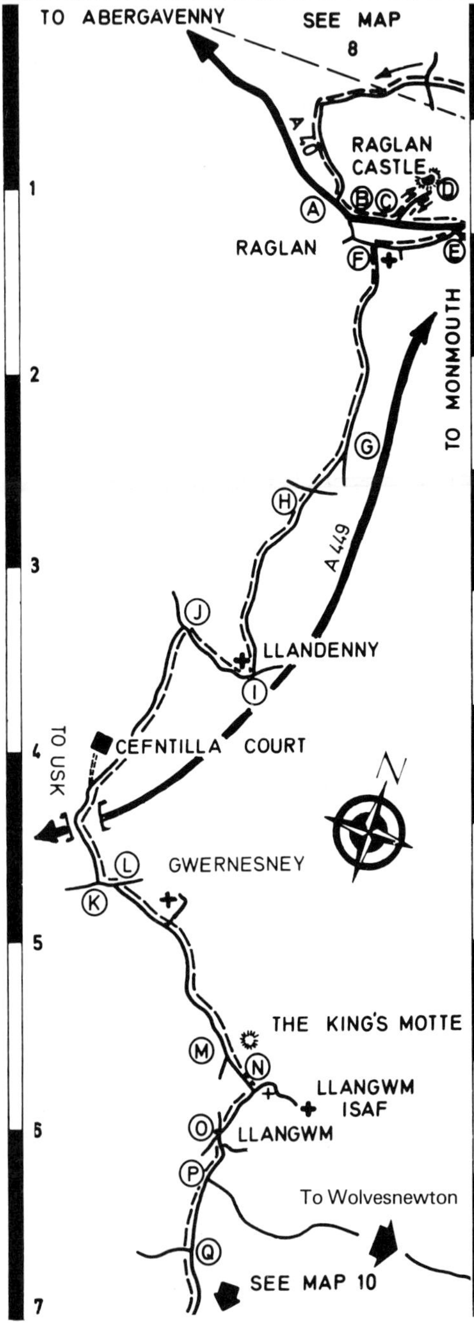

Ref	kms/Miles	Directions	Sign-posted
	1.3	Raglan Castle now visible to left	
A	.7	Turn left on to wider road	Monmouth
B	.1	Bear left on to A40 at large roundabout	Monmouth
C1	.3	Turn left, to visit Raglan Castle	Raglan Castle
D	.2	Arrive Raglan Castle Car Park, and **turnabout**	
C2	.1	Turn left, re-joining A40	No sign
E	.3	Turn right, with care	Raglan
	.4	Raglan entry signed	
F	.1	Turn left at X rds. beyond the church	Llandenny
G	1.2	Fork right up small road (Watch for this carefully)	No sign
H	.3	Over small off-set cross roads	Llandenny
I	1.2	Turn right at T junction, by Llandenny Church	Cefntilla
J	.5	Turn left at T junction	Cefntilla
	.2	Lovely pastoral views from small ridge at entry to Cefntilla Park	
	.6	Cefntilla Court on right	
	.3	Turn left at T junction by entrance to Cefntilla Court	Usk
	.2	Over bridge crossing A449	
K	.3	Turn left at T junction on to B4235, and...	Chepstow
L		Fork right keeping on B4235	Llangwm
	.2	Gwernesney church over to left	
	1.0	Small earthworks on left... Called 'The Kings Motte'	
	.1	Enter Llangwm and...	
M		Turn left off B4235	Church
N	.3	Turn right at T junction by farm. (But turn left and go half a mile to visit old Llangwm church)	No sign
O	.3	Turn left by the Bridge Inn, rejoining B4235 (Keep on B4235 through Llangwm)	No sign
P	.1	Straight, not left (But turn left if you wish to visit Model Farm, Wolvesnewton... 1.5)	Chepstow
Q	.6	Straight, not right	No sign
		Total mileage on this map: 10.9	

CROWN COPYRIGHT RESERVED

On Route

Raglan Castle
Raglan's existing remains date from the 15th century, and further building went on well into the 17th century. Its capture in 1646 by General Fairfax, after a long siege, marked the effective end of the Civil War, and the castle never recovered from the 'dismantling' that followed. However its massive remains had already become a source of interest to 'tourists' by the beginning of the 19th century.
Explore Raglan at leisure, from the great 'Yellow Tower of Gwent', with its ten feet thick walls and deep stone sided moat, to the delicate, empty traceried windows in the great Hall. Sit on green lawns and look out over the gentle landscape of Gwent, once so heavily dominated by this splendid castle.

1. Raglan Castle

Raglan
The 14th century church has a dull interior although there are the tombs of three Earls of Worcester (of Raglan Castle) in a separate chapel. Their disfigurement was probably the work of Fairfax's besieging troops (See above).

Llandenny
Small, sleepy village with a very pleasing church. It has a fine, plain tower, and a long narrow interior, enriched with excellent modern panelling, a stoutly timbered old roof, and an attractive 17th century font. The beautiful lychgate completes this picture of simple perfection.

2. Llandenny Church

Cefntilla Court
Used by Fairfax as his headquarters during the siege of Raglan, Cefntilla was largely rebuilt in the 19th century, and presented to Lord Raglan, in memory of his father, the Crimean War Commander. It is not open to the Public.

Gwernesney Church
Attractive little building tucked away behind a farm, to the left of our road beyond Point L. There are fine views from the churchyard, down to Usk, and to the hill country beyond Cwmbran. Inside there is an interesting 15th century screen around the font, and a good screen of the same period... plenty of atmosphere here.

3. Gwernesney Church

Llangwm Isaf
Delightfully situated in a wooded valley, nearly a mile from the main road. Llangwm Isaf church must not be missed. Walk through the churchyard and up the meadow beyond the brook, to obtain the best view, and then return to look inside at the magnificent medieval screen complete with rood loft.

Wolvesnewton Model Farm Folk Collection
An exhibition in unique cross shaped stone barns, depicting much of the comic and curious side of Victorian life, including a Victorian bedroom, farm carts, country crafts, agricultural implements, etc. Do not miss this.

4. Llangwm Isaf Church

Map 10

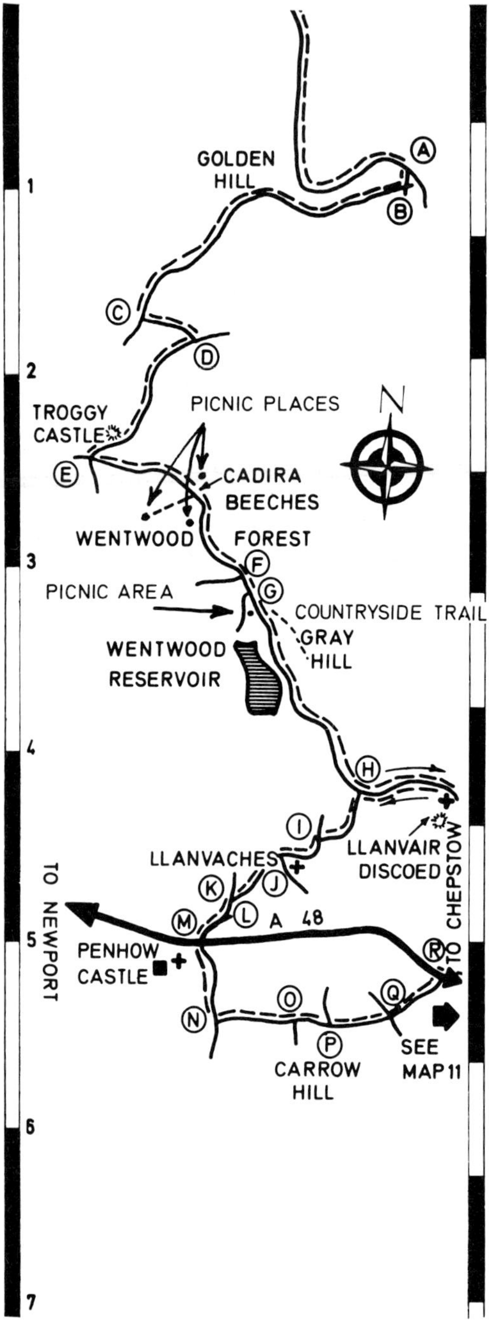

Ref.	Miles/kms	Directions	Sign-posted
A	1.9	Turn right at small X rds by bus stop at top of hill, off B4235. Watch for this carefully	No sign
B	.1	Turn right at another small X rds.	No sign
	.3	Narrow road with holly hedges	
	1.0	Bracken covered slopes, with magnificent views over Vale of Usk	
C	.6	Turn left at T junction by small triangular green	No sign
D	.3	Turn sharp right at T junction	No sign
	.8	Ruins of Troggy Castle in field on right	
E	.2	Turn very sharp left at X rds.	Llanvair Discoed
	.1	Enter Wentwood Forest	
	.4	Pass Cadira Beeches Picnic Place on left. Footpaths into forest on left	
		Track up right to Wentwood Lodge Picnic Place and viewpoint	
	.3	Nine Wells Picnic Place on right	
F	.4	Straight, not right	No sign
G	.1	Straight, not right (Gray Hill Countryside Trail on left. Car Park, Picnic Area, and Viewpoint for Wentwood Reservoir on right)	Newport
H	1.2	Turn sharp right at T junction (But go straight ahead for half a mile to visit Llanvair Discoed church and castle ruins.)	No sign
I	.4	Turn left at T junction and enter Llanvaches	No sign
J	.2	Straight, not left	No sign
K	.4	Bear left at T junction	No sign
L	.1	Bear right on to wider road	No sign
M	.2	Over X rds. with care, crossing A48 (But turn right and then left to visit Penhow church and castle on hill... .4)	St. Bride's
N	.5	Turn left at T junction	Carrow Hill
O	.4	Straight, not right, at entrance to Carrow Hill hamlet	No sign
P	.2	Straight, not left	No sign
Q	.4	Over X rds.	No sign
R	.4	Turn right on to A48	Caerwent
		Total mileage on this map: 11.1	

CROWN COPYRIGHT RESERVED

On Route

Troggy Castle

Ivy clad remains of a small castle upon a thickly wooded mound, visible from the road. Splendidly named but not accessible.

Wentwood Forest

Lies on a 900 foot high ridge from whence there are fine views of the Bristol Channel. Forester's Oaks and Cadira Beeches supply a clue to times past, when Wentwood was known for its oak, elm, sycamore, ash and beech, but today the fast growing softwoods prevail, in response to the insatiable demands of 20th century man. However the Forestry Commission have provided a fine viewpoint and picnic place at Wentwood Lodge (views out over the Bristol Channel), and two other picnic places beside our road (at Cadira Beeches, and Nine Wells). There are pleasant walks eastwards from Cadira Beeches.

Gray Hill

The pleasant walk up the bracken and gorse covered slopes of Gray Hill has now been graced with the title 'Countryside Trail'. This takes in the interesting remains of a Bronze Age stone circle.

There is an excellent picnic area and car park just beyond Point G, which should be used both as a base for the 'trail', and also for its pleasant views out over Wentwood Reservoir. The dry muddy bottom of this reservoir was much photographed by the press during the great drought of summer '76… one of the many that were almost exhausted by the time that rain came in the early autumn.

Llanvair Discoed

Behind the church are the overgrown remains of a castle with two towers and a keep (not open). The church was over-restored in the 19th century but supporting visitors should note the inscription in the porch:

> "Who ever hear on Sunday
> Will practis playing at ball
> It may be before Monday
> The Devil will have you all."

Despite this gloomy warning, we found Llanvair Discoed a pleasant village, with primulas in the churchyard, and borrage on the roadside. The 'Kings Arms' provided bread and cheese, and some of the largest pickled onions we have ever encountered.

Llanvaches

Described by George Borrow as 'a pretty little village', but today only the church deserves mention. This is a low building with a squat saddleback tower. It has a very attractive 17th century south door, and an interesting fragment of Romanesque carving in the porch.

Penhow

The church and castle stand on a small steep hill overlooking the A40. The 13th century church has a pleasant interior with great pillars supporting the tower which rises from the middle of the south aisle.

Continued on Page 23

1. In Wentwood Forest

2. Wentwood Reservoir Picnic Area

3. Wentwood Reservoir

4. Penhow Castle

Map 11

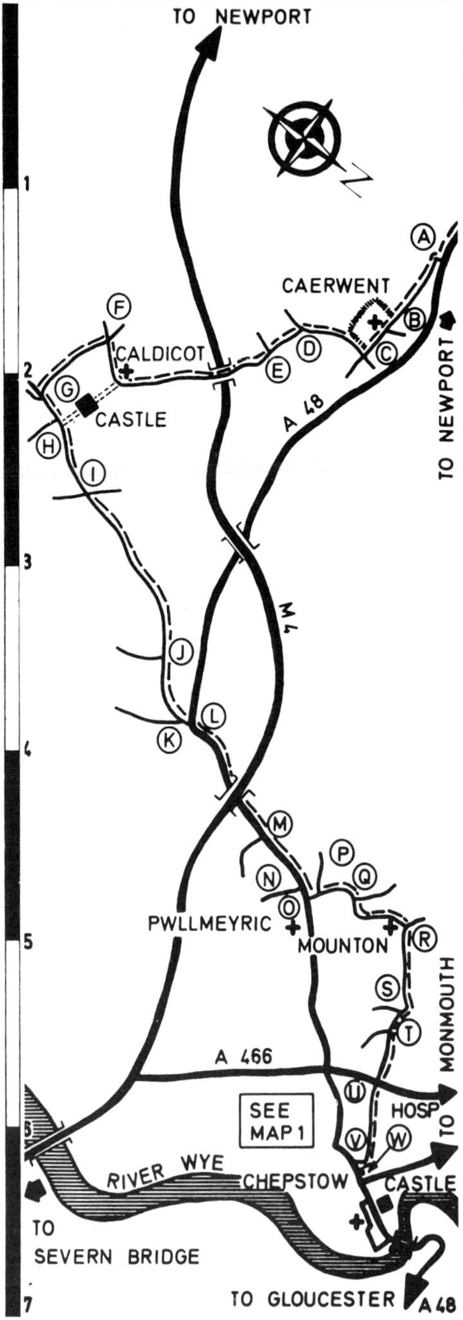

Ref.	kms / Miles	Directions	Sign-posted
A	.8	Turn right, off A48	Caerwent
	.2	Enter Caerwent	
	.2	Path round Roman walls starts here on right	
B	.1	Straight, not left, by the church	No sign
C	.2	Turn right at X rds. beyond the Coach & Horses	No sign
	.1	Roman wall runs alongside road here, path rejoins road	
D	.3	Turn left at T junction	Caldicot Castle & Country Park
E	.2	Straight, not right	No sign
	.2	Cross M4	
	.5	Enter Caldicot	
	.1	Entrance to Castle on left, opposite the church	
F	.2	Turn left at roundabout	Chepstow
G	.5	Turn left at offset X rds.	Chepstow
H	.2	Straight, not right	Chepstow
I	.5	Straight over X rds.	No sign
J	.9	Straight, not right	No sign
K	.5	Straight, not right	No sign
L	.1	Turn right on to A48	Chepstow
	.5	Cross M4	
M	.3	Straight, not right	No sign
N	.3	Straight, not right, at entry to Pwllmeyric	No sign
O	.1	Turn left at T junction, just before New Inn	Shirenewton
P		Almost immediately, straight, not left	No sign
Q	.3	Sharp turn right	No sign
	.3	Mounton church on right	
R	.1	Bear round to right at small roundabout	Chepstow
S	.5	Fork left	No sign
T	.1	Fork left	No sign
U	.3	Over X rds. crossing A466	'Mount Pleasant Hospital'
		Follow down hill into Chepstow	
V	.5	Turn half right by the Green Dragon, and immediately left	No sign
W	.1	Turn left, immediately before reaching Chepstow Gatehouse	'Welsh Street'
		(LINK HERE WITH MAP 1, POINT A)	
		Total mileage on this map: 9.2	

CROWN COPYRIGHT RESERVED

On Route

Penhow Continued from Page 21

The castle, which was the first home in Britain of the famous Seymour family, has a small Norman keep and a 15th century Great Hall. Recent restoration work includes the re-excavation of its ancient rocky moat.

Rock Farm, on the road below, was once the 'Rock and Fountain', a coaching inn where George Borrow is reputed to have stopped. However, Borrow, in the closing stages of his fascinating book 'Wild Wales' only states that he passed through Penhow on his way between Newport and Caerwent. He does however make reference to *two beautiful green hills, the lowest prettily wooded, and having on its top, a fair white mansion called Penhow Castle*. One imagines that Borrow must have been worn out by his travels by this time, and we read that after a further overnight stop at Caerwent, he proceeded to Chepstow, and *having purchased a bottle of port and placing my feet against the sides of the grate I passed my time drinking wine and singing Welsh songs till ten o'clock at night, when I paid my reckoning, amounting to something considerable. Then shouldering my satchel I proceeded to the railroad station, where I purchased a first class ticket, and ensconcing myself in a comfortable carriage was soon on my way to London...* Having read the account of his whole journey, one must agree that Borrow richly deserved both the bottle of port and the first class ticket.

Caerwent

'A poor desolate place consisting of a few old fashioned houses and a strange looking dilapidated church'... So wrote George Borrow more than a hundred years ago. But happily the church is now well cared for and the town is neat and cheerful, if not in itself very exciting.

However it lies upon the Roman town of Venta Silurum, 'the market place of the Silures', which was founded about A.D. 75, as part of the Roman policy of urbanising the native population (The Silures having been previously centred on Llanmelin hill fort, a mile to the N.W.). It was at this time that the headquarters of the 2nd Legion was moved forward from Gloucester to a newly built fortress at Carleon, and the road between ran straight through Caerwent from east to west.

Over the years Caerwent has been systematically excavated, but although the foundations of one or two small buildings are viewable (Turn opposite the church into Pound Lane), the most extraordinary remains are the southern town walls which can be walked all the way from West Gate to East Gate. The walls, which still stand 20 feet high in many places, were constructed in at least three phases: An earthen rampart in the 1st century, a stone wall in the late 2nd century, and the bastions in the mid 4th century.

Caldicot Castle and Country Park
(See Page 25)

1. The South Wall, Caerwent

2. Caldicot Castle

3. Chepstow Bridge

Map 12

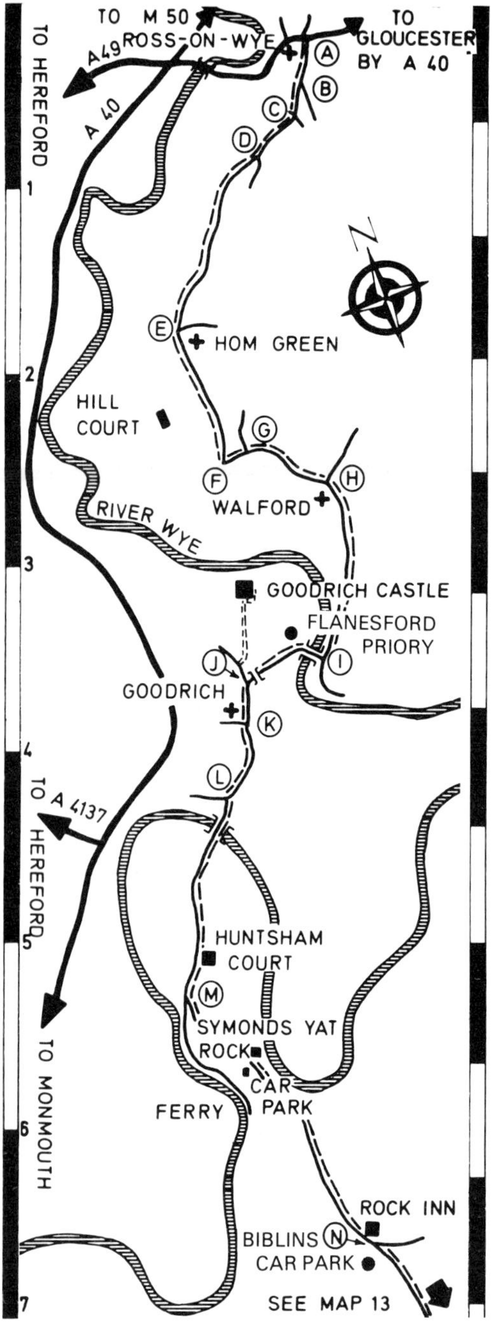

Ref	kms/Miles	Directions	Sign-posted
A		START FROM THE MARKET HALL, ROSS ON WYE, AND TAKE THE B4228 (IF COMING IN FROM MAP 4, TURN LEFT JUST BEFORE MAP 4, JUNCTION B)	Coleford
B	.2	Fork right by the 'Prince of Wales'	'Archenfield Road'
C	.2	Over small X rds. by P.O. Box	No sign
D	.4	Straight, not left	No sign
E	1.0	Bear right at T junction	No sign
	.4	Entrance to Hill Court on right. (Lovely 18th century mansion)	
	.3	Goodrich Castle just visible on bluff ahead	
F	.1	Sharp turn left	No sign
G	.2	Straight, not left	No sign
H	.5	Straight, not left, on to B4228, by Walford Church	No sign
I	1.0	Turn right on to B4229, and immediately cross Kerne Bridge over the Wye	Monmouth
	.2	Flanesford Priory over to right	
	.2	Under bridge at entrance to Goodrich	
J	.1	Straight, not right. (But turn right if you wish to visit Goodrich Castle... very worthwhile)	Symonds Yat
K	.2	Straight, not right, (unless you wish to visit Goodrich Church)	No sign
L	.5	Turn left at T junction	Yat Rock
	.1	Cross Wye, over small bridge	
M	1.0	Fork left. (But fork right to visit riverside)	Yat Rock
		Now climbing all the way to...	
	.9	Main Symonds Yat car park on left. Walk across road from here. Forestry Commission Log Cabin Shop. Forest walks with fantastic views from the Yat Rock	
	.9	Entering semi built-up area of Hillersland. Ugly buildings here	
N	.1	Straight, not left at the Rock Inn	No sign
	.1	Biblins Car Park and Picnic Area on right	
		Total mileage on this map: 8.6	

CROWN COPYRIGHT RESERVED

On Route

Caldicot Castle and Country Park
Splendid medieval castle, extensively renovated by the Cobb family, who purchased it in 1884. See especially the De Bohun Gateway and Keep, and the South Gate. See also the gorgeous white figurehead from Nelson's prize ship, the Foudroyant, and the interesting museum.

Hill Court
Do not miss a glimpse at this handsome early 18th century mansion in mellow brick, in fine parkland to the right of our road beyond Point E.

Walford
Attractive little church looking out over the Wye meadows to Goodrich Castle on its bluff beyond. Its interior has a good Norman arcade, and several pleasant wall monuments.

Flanesford Priory
Here is the refectory of an Augustinian priory, founded here in 1346, and now incorporated into a complex of luxury holiday cottages, which are available on short term lets. A cottage here would make an ideal base for exploring the area covered by this guide.

Goodrich Castle
Situated on a high bluff overlooking the site of a ford across the Wye (Hence Walford... see above), Goodrich castle dates from the 12th and 13th centuries. The massive Norman keep is the oldest part of the castle (1150); the enclosing walls with the towers were built round it some fifty years later, and were extensively reconstructed around 1300.

During the 14th and 15th centuries the castle was one of the favourite residences of the Talbot family, latterly the Earls of Shrewsbury, and it was during this period that Goodrich was in its heyday. It was held by the Royalists in the Civil War, but it fell to the Parliamentarians after a long siege in 1646. Like Raglan, it was so effectively 'dismantled', that it has never been lived in since.

Goodrich with its massive rock cut moat, its shaded lawns, and breath-taking views over the Wye, is our favourite Welsh Border castle.

Symonds Yat
The car park, complete with the Forestry Commission's genuine 'Log Cabin' shop is a very short walk away from the Yat Rock viewpoint. The Rock is probably the most visited point in the whole Wye Valley, and should for this reason be avoided at peak times if at all possible. The views are magnificent... two great sweeps of the Wye encompassing the isthmus on which we stand; and beyond them, stand Goodrich and Ross spires to the north, Whitchurch and the Welsh hills to the west, and the undulating woodlands of Dean Forest to the south and east.

There are two short walks from here, and also a complete Forest Trail, 2½ miles in length. This takes walkers to a spectacular viewpoint looking down in to the Wye Valley and to a 'Forest Garden' (near the car park), with species of all the trees in commercial production in Dean Forest. Guide available from the 'Log Cabin' shop.

1. Ross-on-Wye

2. Kerne Bridge

3. Goodrich Castle

4. The Wye at Symonds Yat

Map 13

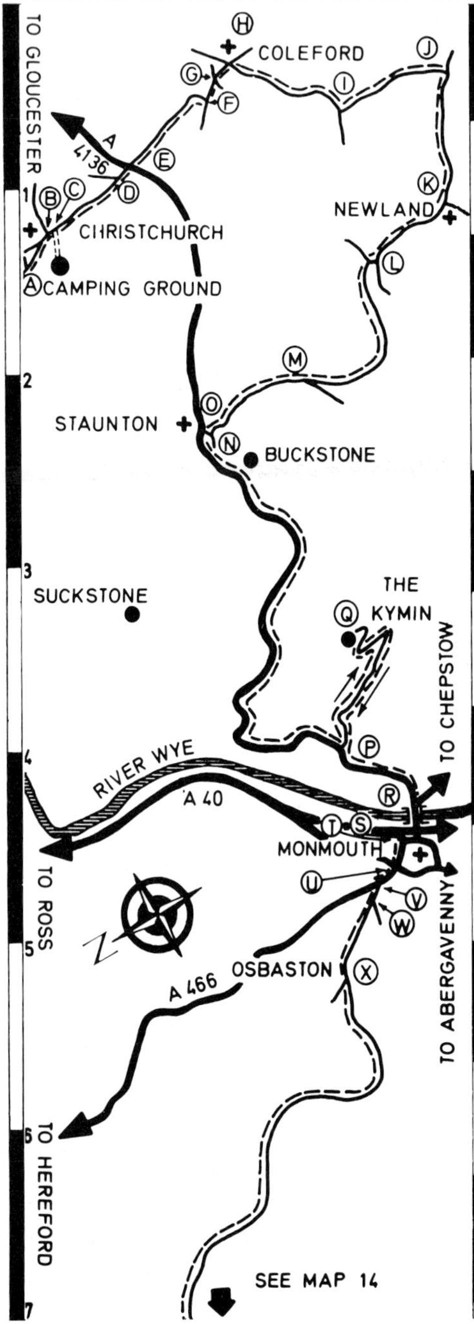

Ref.	kms / Miles	Directions	Sign-posted
A	.5	Fork right, keeping to main road	No sign
	.3	Enter Christchurch	
B	.2	Bear right on to B4228, by Christchurch Church	Coleford
C		Immediately straight, not right, unless you wish to use Christchurch Camp Site	
D	.5	Straight, not left	No sign
E	.1	Over X rds. by the New Inn, crossing A4136	St. Briavels
	.5	Enter Coleford	
F	.2	Turn left at T junction, on to B4431	Coleford
G	.1	Over X rds. at entrance to Coleford	No sign
H	.1	Bear three quarters around main square with tower in centre	Newland
I	.9	Turn left at T junction	Newland
J	.7	Bear right at T junction on to B4231	Newland
K	.5	Straight, not left, at entrance to Newland	No sign
	.3	Ostrich Inn on right, church on left	
L	.6	Turn right and immediately...	Crossways
		Turn left (WATCH FOR THIS 2ND TURN CAREFULLY)	No sign
	.5	Lovely unfenced road through forest	
M	.6	Straight, not left	Staunton
	.6	Enter Staunton	
N	.1	Turn right at T junction	Coleford
O	.1	Turn left on to A4136 by church	No sign
	.9	Gwent entry signed	
P1	2.0	Fork left off A4136 if you wish to visit the Kymin (But go straight into Monmouth if you wish). Climb up steep narrow road with hairpin bends	'The Kymin'
Q	1.4	Arrive at small car park. Footpath to Naval Temple and Roundhouse Descend to point P	
P2	n	Sharp turn left on to A4136	No sign
R	.7	Straight, not left, and...	Monmouth
	.1	Cross River Wye, and...	
		Over traffic lights, at entrance to Monmouth	
S	.1	Turn right at T junction	Town Centre
T	.1	Turn left	Hereford
U	.1	Straight over traffic lights. (But turn left to visit Monmouth)	Hereford
V	.1	Fork left	Osbaston
W	.2	Straight, not left, close to Monnow on left	No sign
X	.3	Fork left	No sign
		Total mileage on this map: 13.3	

CROWN COPYRIGHT RESERVED

On Route

Forest of Dean (See Page 5)

Christchurch Camping Ground
An excellent camp site of 14 acres for tents and caravans, run by the Forestry Commission. The site shop has a good stock of maps and guides.

Coleford
The "Capital of the Forest", is cleaner and brighter than most mining towns we know, but it is not of great interest for visitors. Call at the Forest Office here if you require further information on Forest Trails and other items of interest concerning the Forest of Dean and its wildlife. (Turn left at Point H and left again... Forest Office then on right... Ask for Information Office.)

1. Almshouses, Newland

Newland
The most attractive village in the Forest of Dean, Newland possesses a pleasant inn, 'The Ostrich', a handsome row of white painted almshouses, and an outstanding church. This is often referred to as 'The Cathedral of the Forest' and has a most impressive 14th century tower enriched with five elaborate pinnacles. Internally the great width of the aisles gives an unusually spacious impression, and there is a beautiful series of tombs.

2. Great Castle House, Monmouth

Staunton
Pleasantly situated beneath Highmeadow Woods, Staunton has an interesting church with a central tower and a 15th century stone pulpit.
The 'Buckstone', a massive block of red sandstone from which there are fine views southwards, is easily reached on foot from Staunton (Turn left beyond the 'White Horse'). Opposite the 'White Horse' a track leads to the 'Suckstone', an even larger sandstone block (about one mile from the road).

The Kymin
An 800 foot hill, near the summit of which is a 'Naval Temple', built in 1800, to commemorate British naval heroes, from Hawke to Nelson. It has a slightly Gothick flavour, but at the same time is rather reminiscent of a bus shelter... not very exciting.
However Nelson was entertained here to breakfast, only three years before his death at Trafalgar; and the spectacular views westwards amply justify the long climb up from the main road.

Monmouth
Standing at the confluence of the Wye, Monnow and Trothy, the town of Monmouth is set amidst magnificently wooded hills. Our favourite building in Monmouth is the handsome 18th century Shire Hall, from whence a proud Henry V overlooks pioneer airman, C.S. Rolls in the square (Both natives of Monmouth). But equally interesting are the 13th century gatehouse on the Monnow Bridge, Great Castle House, and the fascinating Nelson Museum in Priory Street.

3. The Monnow Gate, Monmouth

Map 14

kms Ref. Miles		Directions	Sign-posted
	3.2	Through Tregate Castle farmyard. Built on a Motte & Bailey earthwork	
A	.2	Turn right at T junction (But walk down left, to bridge over the Monnow, to idle a few minutes away!)	No sign
B	.3	Turn right at T junction	Welsh Newton
C	1.1	Straight, not right at T junction at top of hill	No sign
D	.3	Turn left on to A466	Hereford
E	.1	Straight, not right by Welsh Newton Church	Hereford
F	.2	Turn left, off A466	Broad Oak
	.6	Through 'The Pleck', a hamlet	
	.3	Splendid view ahead to the Black Mountains	
	.1	Pembridge Castle on right	
G	1.5	Turn left on to B4521, by the Broad Oak Inn	Skenfrith
H	.5	Straight, not right	No sign
	.7	Gwent entry signed. Monnow now visible on left	
I	.4	Turn right by the Priory Motel. (Watch for this carefully) (But go straight ahead to visit Skenfrith church and castle... both well worthwhile)	No sign
	.3	Road now alongside River Monnow	
		Picnic possibilities here.	
		Lovely valley with fine views ahead towards the Black Mountains	
J	1.2	Straight, not right	No sign
	.3	Garway Church on right.	
		Note dovecot beyond the farm	
K	.1	Turn left at T junction in Garway	No sign
	.3	Bracken covered slopes of Garway Hill ahead	
	2.2	Grosmont church and castle ruins on hill top now visible to left across the Monnow	
	.9	Enter Kentchurch village	
L	.1	Straight, not left, by the church. Entrance to Kentchurch Court on right	
M	.1	Turn left at T junction	No sign
		(You are now on the Main Circle Route, just beyond Map 7, Point 1, to which you should now turn)	
		Total mileage on this map: 15.0	

JOIN MAIN ROUTE AT MAP 7 POINT ①

CROWN COPYRIGHT RESERVED

On Route

Welsh Newton

The church has a lovely 14th century stone screen with pointed arches and ball-flower ornaments. There are some attractive 18th century tombstones in the churchyard, and a medieval cross marking the grave of John Kemble, a Roman Catholic priest, who in 1678 was hanged at the age of 80 for saying mass at Pembridge Castle.

1. The Monnow, from Tregate Bridge

Pembridge Castle

A small but interesting 13th century moated castle, with squat gatehouse and a round keep. It appears almost to grow out of the sloping hillside, from whence there are wonderful views up the Monnow valley.

The Broad Oak Inn

It was too early in the morning to stop at this attractively decorated inn when we came this way last, but it now looks very appetising. It advertises a 'restaurant with bar' and 'delicious home-made food', and reports indicate that this claim is fully justified.

2. Pembridge Castle

Skenfrith

A highly attractive village on the Monmouthshire bank of the Monnow, Skenfrith appears to be surrounded on every side by sloping fields and woodlands. A few yards upstream from the bridge is a mill with a brimming weir, overlooked on one side by a broad meadow, and on the other by the church and the castle ruins.

Skenfrith castle is the third member of the 'Trilateral' (See Page 15), and is certainly the cosiest of the three, with green lawns and young trees beside its grey bastions.

The church has a typically 'Welsh Border' tower, and is supported with massive buttresses. Its interior is spacious and entirely unspoilt. Note especially the lovely barrel vaulted roof, the Jacobean box pews, the Altar tomb of Sir John Morgan, and the well known 'Skenfrith Cope'.

3. Skenfrith Castle

Garway

Church, farm and dovecot look out over the utterly peaceful Monnow valley. The fine border tower is only joined to the rest of the church by a narrow passage. Inside there is an excellent barrel vaulted roof and a lovely Norman chancel arch. The 14th century circular dovecote is believed to have belonged to the Knight's Templar who had a commandery here. The dovecote is open daily from 10 to 3.30 all the year. The foundations of the circular church built by the Knights Templar can be seen on the north side of the church.

4. Up the Monnow Valley

Map 15

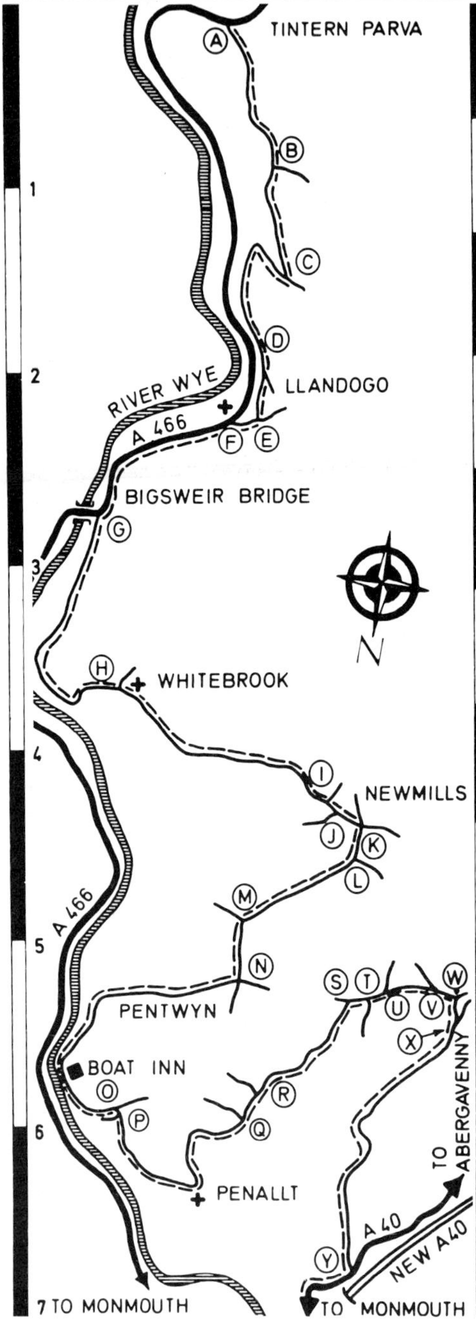

Ref.	kms / Miles	Directions	Sign-posted
		Start from Map 1, Junction E... At Tintern Parva	
A		Turn left, off A466, just before the Wye Valley Hotel	Catbrook
B	.9	Straight, not left at T junction	Trelleck
C	.6	Turn right	Llandogo
D	.9	Straight, not left	No sign
	.1	Enter Llandogo	
	.2	Footpath to Cleiddon Falls on left	
E	.1	Fork right	No sign
F	.1	Turn left on to A466	Monmouth
	.6	Good views of St. Briavels Castle on skyline, up right	
G	.4	Straight, not right, leaving A466 just before it crosses Bigsweir Bridge	Whitebrook
H	1.6	Straight, not left in Whitebrook	No sign
	.6	The Crown on left	
	.6	Into the Newmills area... pools, woods, streams and mills (See opposite)	
I	.4	Straight, not left	No sign
J	.1	Straight, not right	No sign
K	.1	Turn right at X rds.	Penallt
L	.2	Straight not left	No sign
M	.7	Bear left at Y junction by bus shelter	Penallt
N	.3	Turn right at X rds.	'Lone Lane'
		Down steep hill... towards the Wye	
	1.3	The Boat Inn on left, river on right	
O	.5	Turn right, and almost immediately...	Penallt Church
P		Straight, not right	No sign
	.7	Penallt church on right	
Q	.7	Straight, not left	No sign
R	.2	Straight, not left	No sign
S	.8	Turn right at T junction	No sign
T	.2	Straight, not right	No sign
U	.1	Straight, not left	No sign
V	.3	Straight, not left	No sign
W	.3	Turn right at T junction	No sign
X	.2	Bear right on to B4293	Monmouth
Y	1.8	Turn right on to the 'old' A40	Monmouth
	.5	Over the 'new' A40, which is in tunnel below	
	.1	Enter Monmouth	
	.1	Turn left at T junction	Rockfield
	.2	Turn right at roundabout	Town centre
	.1	Cross Monnow by fortified bridge	
Z	.2	Arrive main square, Monmouth	
		Note: Bear left and left again at traffic lights, to place yourself just beyond Map 13, Junction U	
		Total mileage on this map: 16.8	

CROWN COPYRIGHT RESERVED

On Route

Tintern Forest

The road between Tintern Parva and Llandogo passes through some of the loveliest parts of Tintern Forest, including stands of Norway Spruce, Western Red Cedars, Sitka Spruce, and larches over 100 feet tall. In a few places the Wye can be glimpsed through the trees, hundreds of feet below.

1. The Wye, from Tintern Forest

Llandogo

Clings to the hillside above a pleasant bend in the Wye, and has several shops and restaurants. However the 700 foot high Cleiddon Shoots waterfall is the only item of real interest in Llandogo, whose charms appear to have been over-stressed in some guides.

Bigsweir

Attractive Bigsweir House is visible across the river ½ mile beyond Point F), and although we do not cross it, spare a moment to look at Thomas Telford's handsome iron bridge, with the little tollhouse at its western end. (Telford's greatest work was the Menai Straits Road Bridge).

2. Bigsweir Bridge

Whitebrook and Newmills

Fascinating little wooded valley with a hamlet at each end, Whitebrook at the foot, Newmills at the head. In the 16th century a wire-works was established here; no doubt drawing heavily upon the surrounding woodlands for fuel. With the coming of the Industrial Revolution, these were moved to the coal bearing areas of the Black Country and South Wales, but the clear waters of the White Brook were put to better use, when several paper mills were built here in the early 19th century (hence New Mills). Now the paper makers have also gone, but many of their beautiful mill pounds have been put to good use, for the breeding of trout.

3. House at Newmills

Penallt

Has a few houses and a church, perched on a high bracken covered hillside, overlooking the Wye. The church has a small saddleback tower, and a fine old door (dated 1539).

It seems appropriate to round off our tour of the quieter corners of the Wye valley at this peaceful hamlet, overlooking the busy main road hundreds of feet below us.

4. Penallt Church

INDEX

	Page
Abbots Wood Trail	7
Abenhall	7
Aconbury	13
ARICONIUM	9
Beaufort family	3
Bigsweir	31
Black Mountains	14, 17, 28
Blackpool Bridge	7
Blaize Bailey Viewpoint	7
Bolstone	13
Borrow, George	21, 23
Brampton Abbotts	9
Bristol Channel	21
Broadmoor Common	10
Broad Oak Inn	29
Brockhampton	11
Brockweir	3
Buckstone, The	27
Cadira Beeches	20
Caerwent	23
Caldicot Castle	23
Cannop Ponds	5
Canute, King	5
Capler, Camp	10
Capler Woods	10
Carleon	23
Carrow Hill	20
'Cathedral of the Forest'	27
Cefntilla Court	19
Chepstow	3, 22
Christchurch Camping Ground	27
Clearwell Caves Iron Mines	5
Cleiddon Shoots Waterfall	31
Coldharbour	2
Coleford	27
Dean, Forest of	5
Dean Forest Railway	5
Dean Heritage Centre	4, 7
Dean, Little	7
Dewchurch, Little	13
Dewchurch, Much	13
Fairfax, General	19
Flanesford Priory	25
Flaxman, John	17
Forest Office, Coleford	27
Forest Trails	7
Fownhope	11
Foy	11
Garway	29
Garway Hill	28
Glendower, Owen	15
Gloucester	23
Goodrich Castle	25
Graig Syfyrddin	14, 17
Gray Hill	21
Great Castle House	27
Green Bottom	6
Green Man, The	11
Gregory, Sir William	11
Grosmont Castle	15
Gwernesney	19
Haugh Wood	10
Hen Gwrt	17

	Page
Henry V	27
Highmeadow Woods	27
Hill Court	25
Hillersland	24
Hoaldalbert	14
'Hole-in-the-Wall'	10
Holme Lacy	13
Hostry Inn, The	17
How Caple	11
Kemble, John	29
Kentchurch	15, 28
Kentchurch Court	15
Kilpeck	15
King's Motte, The	18
Knights Templar	29
Kymin, The	27
Kyrle, John	9
Lethaby, W. R.	11
Llandenny	19
Llandogo	31
Llangwm Isaf	19
Llanmelin Hill Fort	23
Llantilio Crossenny	17
Llanvaches	21
Llanvair Discoed	21
Lugg, River	11
Lydney	5
Mitcheldean	7
Monmouth	27, 30
Monnow Bridge	27
Monnow, River	14, 15, 27, 29
Mordiford	11
Morgan, Sir John	29
Mounton	22
Nash, John	15
Naval Temple	27
Nelson, Admiral	23, 27
Nelson Museum	27
'New Fancy View'	5
Newland	27
Newmills	31
Offa's Dyke Footpath	17
Orepool	4
Osbaston	26
Parkend	5
Pembridge Castle	29
Penallt	31
Penhow	21, 23
Penhow Castle	21, 23
Penrhos	17
Pentwyn	16
Penyard Hill	9
Pleck, The	28
Pugin, A.	3
Pwllmeyric	22
Pye, Walter	13
Raglan	19
Raglan Castle	19
Raglan, Lord	19
Rhys the Terrible	15
Rolls, C. S.	27
Roman Road	7
Ross-on-Wye	9, 24